Original title:
Saturn's Ring Rhymes

Copyright © 2025 Creative Arts Management OÜ
All rights reserved.

Author: Natalia Harrington
ISBN HARDBACK: 978-1-80567-790-1
ISBN PAPERBACK: 978-1-80567-911-0

Ballet of the Mansions

In the sky, the giants dance,
With a twirl and a silly prance.
One wears a hat too big to fit,
While others laugh and never quit.

There's a moon that trips on a star,
Spinning round with a wobbling jar.
They all giggle, float, and glide,
As comets join in, eyes open wide.

Rings made of candy floss delight,
Twinkling brightly in the night.
A squirrel jokes from a lunar view,
Saying, "Why don't we try a new move too?"

Jumping jests in a cosmic spree,
Galaxies wink in harmony.
With a whoop, they leap into space,
All together in this zany race!

Echoes in the Ether

In a cosmic game of tag,
Planets chase with a wag.
Jupiter laughs, spins around,
While tiny moons hop, confound.

Stars wink like twinkling eyes,
As comets zoom with surprise.
Galaxies swirl in a spree,
Gallivanting through the cosmic sea.

Celestial Serenade

Whispers echo through the void,
Each twinkle is a cosmic ploy.
Uranus spins in a silly way,
While Venus dances, bright as day.

Mars juggles with asteroids,
Making music, never avoids.
Mercury zips, quick as a wink,
In a comic twist, they all link.

Glistening Halo Melodies

Rings are flinging, wildly swayed,
Like confetti at a grand parade.
Particles play in a frolicsome glide,
As Saturn grins with a cosmic pride.

Bouncing tunes on a solar breeze,
The planets frolic, doing as they please.
Asteroids tap on a celestial drum,
While starlight giggles, saying, "Come!"

Rhythms of the Planetary Dance

Cosmic creatures twirl and spin,
A ballet in space, where all begin.
Ceres twirls in a tutu made of ice,
Pluto joins in, not thinking twice.

The Sun claps, lighting the floor,
While meteorites skate and roar.
Dancing rings make a joyful song,
In the galaxy where we all belong.

Whirling Whispers

Round and round in cosmic play,
The little rocks dance all day.
They bump and giggle, oh what fun,
A merry charade under the sun.

If you should listen close with glee,
You'd hear them chant a harmony.
Rolling laughter fills the space,
As they twirl in a shimmering race.

Celestial Enigma

A riddle spun in starry night,
Why do the rings shine so bright?
They're just a bunch of dust and grime,
Getting their groove on, keeping time.

Little moons skip and hop about,
What's this wisdom all about?
They chuckle and wave from afar,
Wiggling their moons, a cosmic bazaar.

Bands of Silence

In the silence of the cosmic sea,
Giggles echo endlessly.
A giant wheel with sparkly bits,
Making waves and funny quips.

The rocks abide, a catchy crew,
Playing tag, oh what a view!
They shift and slide, without a care,
In this round dance, life's a fair.

Rhythm of the Cosmos

Feel the pulse, the cosmic beat,
Where little pebbles tap their feet.
Dancing close in a swirling spree,
Creating tunes for you and me.

In the void, they laugh and tease,
Making music on the breeze.
Their anthem rises, light and free,
Oh, what a sight, come dance with me!

Cosmic Chords

In the galaxy of giggles, we fly,
Where planets wear hats, oh my, oh my!
The sun's doing the cha-cha, quite a sight,
And moons are moonwalking, holding on tight.

With comets as carry-ons, zooming around,
Stars keep tripping on stardust, safe and sound.
Nebulas are painting, oh what a show,
While black holes are dancing, 'Don't fall, oh no!'

Celestial Sketches

The universe doodles with a quirky pen,
Drawing smiley asteroids again and again.
A rocket went shopping for glitter and fun,
While the Milky Way giggles, 'Come here, my son!'

Satellites spin like tops, all around,
Echoing laughter with a joyful sound.
Galaxies engage in a playful race,
As meteors tumble with style and grace.

The Whispering Bands

Rings of laughter twirl like frolicsome bling,
Asteroids whisper secrets, oh, what do they bring?
Cosmic clowns juggling stars without a care,
Satellites chuckle, 'Look, I'm flying through air!'

Comets wear bowties, so dapper, so neat,
While planets do ballet, tapping their feet.
A cosmic parade, such a glorious sight,
With laughter echoing through the starry night.

Interstellar Imagery

In a portrait of chaos, colors collide,
Planets make faces, and stars choose to hide.
A spaceship trips over moonbeams, oh dear,
And the sun shouts, 'Watch out!' with laughter and cheer.

Galactic jesters toss stardust in style,
Zooming through space with a sparkly smile.
Singularity twirls in a cosmic delight,
As constellations giggle throughout the night.

Enigmatic Orbits

In the cosmic dance of stray cats,
Planets chase their colorful hats.
Around and round they swiftly swoop,
While comets join the funky loop.

Galaxies twirl like disco balls,
Alien ducks heed the call.
Stars giggle, lighting up the skies,
As black holes joke with playful sighs.

Twilight's Rings

At twilight's edge the rings do swing,
Rocky pebbles play and sing.
They twirl and twist in a silly cheer,
While meteorites sip cosmic beer.

A dance-off starts between the moons,
With space-time beats and funny tunes.
They shimmy through the velvet night,
Tripping over starlight, what a sight!

Echoing Celestial Moons

Moons echo laughter in the void,
Dodging asteroids, never annoyed.
With silly faces, they chase each other,
Causing a ruckus, like no other.

Orbiting planets giggle and sway,
In a playful game, they all play.
With each spin, they make a fuss,
Creating chaos, just for us.

Universe in Verse

In the universe, where jokes roam free,
Stars throw puns like confetti.
Planets tease with their orbits wide,
Inviting laughter from every side.

With quirky satellites acting strange,
Galactic giggles twist and change.
While cosmic winds blow funny tales,
The sky erupts in joyous gales.

Cosmic Canvas

In a galaxy far, they paint with cheer,
A brush made of stardust, it's all so clear.
With wobbly planets doing a funny jig,
Even black holes spin in a cosmic pig.

Comets with tails like a dog in a chase,
Throwing sparkles and giggles across the space.
Nebulas giggle, they dance with delight,
Winking at astronauts lost in their flight.

Stellar Sentences

An asteroid texted, 'I'm feeling quite rocky,'
While moons clapped their hands, said, 'A bit of a jockey!'
Planets replied with a chuckle and glee,
'Let's orbit in circles, it's funny, you see!'

Dark matter whispers secrets in jest,
While quasars joke around, having fun is the quest.
Galaxies swirling, a comedic parade,
The universe giggles, and it's all home-made.

Astral Echoes

In the vacuum, they echo with laughter and grace,
Stars telling stories, each one has a face.
They twinkle in rhythm, a universal band,
Creating a cosmos that's whimsically planned.

Supernovae pop like the grandest confetti,
While aliens dance, say, 'Isn't this zesty?'
With laughter contagious, they bring pure delight,
The expanse of the cosmos, a jovial sight.

Dancing in the Void

In the void where the dark meets the light,
Quasars bounce along, what a fanciful sight!
Gravity's a prankster, keeps messing their dance,
While planets do pirouettes, lost in a trance.

Asteroids shimmy, they roll with great flair,
Each twist and each turn shedding starlight in air.
Comedic collisions, a cosmic ballet,
In the vastness of space, come laugh and play!

Jewel of the Night Sky

Twinkling bright in a velvet veil,
A hula hoop lost, what a tale!
With icy rocks and dust galore,
Who knew space could be such a chore?

Little dancers in a cosmic show,
Spinning around with a playful flow.
A celestial party, no doubt in sight,
Who knew space could be this light?

Spinning Dreams in the Void

In the stillness of the cosmic sea,
Dancing particles, just you and me.
Like a merry-go-round, spinning all night,
Bumping into stars, oh what a sight!

Floating on laughter, in zero-g fun,
Watch out for comets, they sure like to run!
In this dreamy patch of the great unknown,
We're making wishes on pebbles we've thrown.

Harmonies of the Heavenly Band

Listen close to the giggles above,
A chorus of planets serenading love.
Jupiter sings with a booming voice,
While Mars plays the flute, oh what a choice!

The stars bop along to the cosmic beat,
Comets can't help but tap their feet.
With each note, the universe grins,
Guess it's true, music really spins!

Cosmic Lace

A pattern of dust, so fine and frail,
Like grandma's doilies, it won't fail.
Woven in magic, stitched with delight,
What happens in space stays out of sight!

Fluffy clouds twirl like a slow dance,
Gravity's grip puts us in a trance.
As we twinkle and swirl with the stars above,
Remember, the cosmos is filled with love!

Aurora's Embrace

In the skies, the colors twirl,
A dancing light, a cosmic swirl.
She giggles bright as she spins around,
Painting rainbows without a sound.

Her laughter echoes, makes stars blush,
Even comets pause in a rush.
With a wink, she lights the night,
Bubbles in space, what a sight!

Chronicles of Celestial Bodies

Jupiter's storms are quite a chat,
He tells wild tales while I sit flat.
Mars just nods as if to say,
'Wait for me, I'll ride the rays!'

Venus struts, all dressed in style,
She twirls in clouds, oh what a smile!
Mercury zips, a flash of light,
'Catch me if you can!'—a funny flight!

Cosmic Voyage

Zooming past the moons we fly,
With popcorn planets floating by.
Galaxies giggle in their dance,
Who knew space could put us in a trance?

Asteroids tease with a cheeky grin,
They dodge the ships like it's a win.
Nebulas puff, thinking they're grand,
'Hold my drink, this is unplanned!'

Fragments of the Universe

Stardust falls like confetti bright,
Each piece whispers tales of delight.
Planets play peek-a-boo with the sun,
Who's hiding now? It's all in fun!

The black holes joke, 'What's the rush?'
While light-years play a cosmic hush.
With every twinkle, laughter rings,
In the void, joy still sings!

Stardust Symphonies

In the night, the stars collide,
Dancing gems on a cosmic ride.
Jupiter sways, a big round guy,
While Mars insists, he's a little shy.

Moonbeams giggle as they play,
Comets zoom in a wild ballet.
Nebulas swirl in a cloud of blue,
While Pluto jokes, 'I'm still with you!'

Celestial Mirage

A twinkling space with a wink so bright,
Galaxies twist in a silly flight.
Planets pop like fizzy drinks,
As asteroids bounce, what do you think?

Venus wears a polka dot dress,
While Saturn laughs, 'Oh, what a mess!'
Stars giggle as they twirl around,
Comets snicker, a merry sound.

The Dreams of a Giant

A giant once dreamed of candy skies,
With chocolate rains and pie so high.
His laughter echoed through the void,
While shooting stars danced, overjoyed.

He sprinkled stardust on his toes,
While Saturn's cousin threw some bows.
In this dreamland where giggles reign,
The universe bursts with wacky gain!

Harmony in Motion

In the cosmos, a jolly tune,
With dancing planets under the moon.
Stars tap their heels, all aglow,
In a waltz that steals the show.

Neptune cracks a joke, quite absurd,
While Venus hums a silly word.
With each spin, the fun expands,
As space-time wobbles and laughs in bands.

Verses of the Unknown

In the cosmos where giggles bloom,
Stars dance in miniature rooms.
Planets wear hats of glittering light,
Juggling moons in the dark of night.

A comet trips on a space-bound loop,
Giggling asteroids join in the troop.
Black holes hide in the corners of night,
Throwing confetti that sparkles so bright.

Ethereal Ribbons

With ribbons of gas, the universe plays,
Tickling planets in silly ways.
A star winks at a wandering star,
As it spins round in a celestial bazaar.

The comets race on a lollipop path,
Chasing stardust and vibrations of math.
Space suits with polka dots all around,
As laughter echoes where voids are found.

Celestial Melancholy

A planet sighs, feeling a bit blue,
As it spins slowly, not knowing what to do.
But a moon rolls by with a chuckle so grand,
Saying life in the cosmos is just out of hand!

The stars join in with a twinkling tune,
While the sun plays peek-a-boo, all afternoon.
A nebula shrugs, embracing the chill,
Turning sadness into a cosmic thrill.

Cosmic Aurora

With colors that dance like socks on a line,
The universe giggles with every design.
Bright beams of laughter shoot through the night,
Painting the heavens with sheer delight.

A quasar spins, wearing a silly grin,
While space-time stretches to let the fun in.
Galaxies swirl in a vibrant embrace,
As the cosmos joins in a playful race.

Celestial Whispers

In the night sky, donuts float,
Planets wearing silly coats.
Wobbling stars in a playful dance,
Comets twirl in a cosmic trance.

Asteroids giggle, rolling by,
With bouncy moons that never lie.
Nebulae sprout like cotton candy,
A universe that's just too dandy.

Galaxies spin in a goofy race,
Black holes laughing in the space.
Gravity's pull, a cheeky trick,
Making stardust giggle, oh so quick.

Supernovae burst with a chuckle,
In the cosmos, we all huddle.
Each twinkle tells a funny tale,
In this vast place where dreams set sail.

Cosmic Looping Lullabies

Hopping planets, having a spree,
Rings of laughter, can you see?
Whirling galaxies play tag at night,
Cosmic giggles take their flight.

Moons with hats and starry shoes,
Where do they go? Who even knew?
Shooting stars throw wishes in the air,
Wandering starlings without a care.

Pulsars chime with silly tunes,
Dancing meteors with golden spoons.
A universe where all is bright,
Turning chaos into lighthearted delight.

Celestial beings in a gleeful mix,
Astrobiologists throwing quick tricks.
In this cosmic comedy show, we cheer,
As space sings sweet lullabies in our ear.

Orbital Odes

Around and around in the sky so high,
Silly satellites give a wink and a sigh.
Twinkling lights in a backstage role,
As comets carry on, oh what a stroll!

The moon wears shades, looking so fine,
Stars flex muscles, oh how they shine!
Planets jive in an orbital spin,
Lost in the laughter that bubbles within.

Every space pebble has a prank to pull,
Meteor showers are a laugh, oh so full.
With each clap of thunder in the black,
Celestial giggles always pull us back.

Take a ride on the cosmic funfair,
The universe invites, with style and flair.
Buckle up tight, the laughs won't stop,
In the stellar kingdom, we all hop!

Threads of the Celestial Belt

Laughter threads through the starry seams,
 Asteroids play tricks, or so it seems.
  With cosmic yarn in a pastel hue,
   Knitting moments, oh what a view!

Planets wear socks, mismatched delight,
 Capes made of stardust, swirling bright.
  Nebulae giggle as they drift and sway,
   In a fabric of frolic, they weave and play.

Jupiter's grin, a giant's embrace,
 As Mercury zips at a wild pace.
  The comical cosmos, a whimsical ride,
   On stardust trails, we laugh and slide.

The universe whispers secrets and cheer,
 A tapestry woven, our joys draw near.
  In this canvas of laughter, we all belong,
   Singing together, the eternal song.

Cosmic Cascades

In space, where the jokes are vast,
Stars twinkle like they're having a blast.
Planets roll like a cosmic game,
While comets pass, whispering names.

Puns float by on cosmic streams,
Galaxies giggle at punny dreams.
Asteroids dance with a silly bounce,
While light-years laugh in a vast flounce.

Voids hold secrets, very cheeky,
Einstein's hair looks quite streaky.
Nebulas swirl in colors so bright,
Making space feel quite light-hearted tonight.

So if you're lost in the cosmic play,
Join the laughter—don't drift away!
In this universe, full of delight,
Every star shares a joke each night.

Lyrical Landscapes

In the cosmos where quirks collide,
Planets sing, their tunes set aside.
Galactic choruses—what a scene,
Satellites shimmy like they've just seen a queen.

Peeking in through the lunar glow,
Little moons giggle in a row.
Each comet's tail, a brush of delight,
Painting smiles on the canvas of night.

Stardust tap-dances in twinkling boots,
Galaxies twirl in fancy suits.
Cosmic echoes bounce with glee,
As constellations sneak in for tea.

In every corner, a story's looped,
Making us laugh, we're all grouped.
So here's to the fun, bright as a spark,
In this lyrical space, we make our mark.

Dreams of the Night Sky

Nighttime whispers play in my mind,
Where silly thoughts are easy to find.
Stars don hats, and moons wear shoes,
In this theater of cosmic news.

Dreams float like balloons from the past,
With punchlines flying far and fast.
Satellites giggle, laughing so bright,
Creating magic that's pure delight.

How do the galaxies regain their poise?
With playful banter and heavenly noise.
Asteroids rolling, pirouettes in flight,
Make even black holes feel light tonight.

So rest your head, let humor unfold,
In dreamland where the stars are bold.
As cosmos chuckles, don't let it fade,
In nightly adventures, joy is made.

The Divinity of Distance

From far away, the sun sends a wink,
Tickling the Earth, making us think.
Planets stretch in a rubbery fun,
While black holes hide, playing stun-gun.

Light-years travel at a comic pace,
Filling the voids with smiles to embrace.
Each comet tails like a feathered friend,
Waving at you as they loop and bend.

Distances laugh, they stretch and yawn,
While daydreams dance on the cosmic lawn.
Jokes travel faster than light, we say,
In the universe's jestful play.

So revel in space with laughter in tow,
Where distances shrink in the cosmic glow.
In every twinkle, a chuckle resides,
As the universe plays with shimmering tides.

Orbiting Harmonies

In the sky, the planets twirl,
With giggles that make comets whirl.
Jupiter laughs at Mars's cheer,
While Saturn spins with rings so dear.

Asteroids dance with a comic twist,
In this vast space, who can resist?
Galaxies chuckle, stars do play,
Creating funny games each day.

Shooting stars race, what a sight!
Wishing wells in the velvet night.
Space is a place of bubbly fun,
Where laughter echoes, never done.

With each orbit, a chuckle's found,
In this realm, joy knows no bound.
The universe grins, a playful page,
A cosmic joke, all ages engage.

Nebula's Embrace

In a cloud where colors blend,
A cosmic giggle has no end.
Stars poke fun at each other's glow,
In swirling hues, they steal the show.

Wobbling planets play hide and seek,
While space dust tickles, oh-so-sneak.
Galactic pranks in vibrant displays,
Creating laughter in swirling ways.

Astro-bunnies hop through the haze,
With glittering tails in funny ways.
In a nebula where jokes take flight,
Who knew stardust could be so bright?

Through the giggles of cosmic art,
Nebula's embrace warms every heart.
In the universe's grand ballet,
A giggle echoes every day.

Cosmic Lullabies

Beneath the stars, a sleepy tune,
Laughter whispers by the moon.
Comets hum their silly rhymes,
Cradled in the waves of time.

Crickets chirp in cosmic space,
Bouncing jokes at a merry pace.
While meteors paint the night with glee,
Cozy dreams float joyously.

Planets snore with a gentle sway,
In dreamy worlds where the stars play.
Galaxies giggle in their sleep,
Lullabies that the cosmos keep.

As lullabies of joy unfold,
In cosmic tales, the laughter's told.
A nighttime ballet of jester skies,
Where every twinkle fun implies.

Rings of Time

A hula hoop in cosmic dance,
With every spin, it takes a chance.
Rings of laughter spin around,
In wobbly joy, they are found.

Time spins tales of giggly grace,
In endless loops through outer space.
Jupiter's giants leap and dash,
In a time-warping, playful crash.

Waltzing orbits with a merry cheer,
Comets join in without a fear.
Each twirl a story to remember,
In the atomic joke that's tender.

Rings of time, a cosmic jest,
Where laughter soars above the rest.
With each revolution, joy entwines,
In the universe, where humor shines.

Glistening Bands of Wonder

In cosmic loops, they play a game,
Twinkling hard, they call your name.
With ice and dust, they dance around,
A ring of laughs, no frowns are found.

Whirl like a dancer in the night,
Spinning tales in pure delight.
They twiddle and they twirl so bright,
Warming hearts with their jovial light.

What secrets do these rings keep tight?
Maybe jokes that cause a fright?
They giggle softly, float and swing,
In the universe, they reign as king!

So come on out, do not stay shy,
Join the jesters in the sky.
With glistening bands, all join the fun,
With laughter echoing, we're never done!

Planetary Poetry

Around the globe, the verses fly,
With quirky twists that never lie.
A cosmic sonnet spins a tale,
Of merry quips that can't grow stale.

Planets gather, share a grin,
With rhymes and jests that swirl within.
A merry band of celestial buffoons,
Singing sweetly, over the moons.

Galactic giggles bounce around,
From cratered surfaces to starlit ground.
Eclipsing sorrows with friendly pings,
Every verse is stitched with zing.

So toss your frown to the starry dust,
Join this party, laugh you must!
With planetary spells in our sights,
We'll weave the cosmos with our delights!

Stardust Serenades

In a cosmic bubble, tunes arise,
With stardust sprinkled, oh what a prize!
Melodies dance on twinkling beams,
As laughter floats in fading dreams.

Wobbling planets raise a cheer,
With comets zooming, drawing near.
Silly verses, they swirl and tease,
Bringing joy with playful ease.

Galaxies giggle in a rhyming spree,
Shooting stars hum in harmony.
Songs of whimsy fill the night,
As echoes twinkle, oh what a sight!

So spark your soul with cosmic sound,
Let joy and laughter be unbound.
In a serenade of stardust bright,
We find our rhythm, hearts take flight!

Celestial Curved Echoes

In a spiral dance, the echoes rise,
Bouncing off planets, oh what a surprise!
Curvy whispers in the void,
Damage laughter, never destroyed.

Twinkling choirs in a celestial hall,
Each note bounces, making us all.
Gravity's grip can't dim their glee,
In cosmic chambers, they flow free.

Giggles ride the cosmic waves,
Crafting memories that laughter saves.
Echoes twinkle, dance, and play,
As time ticks by in the milky spray.

So join the mirth, don't stay aloof,
Even stars delight in a good goof!
With echoes curving through the night,
Laughter and joy take endless flight!

Enchanted Celestial Ribbons

In the sky, where jesters play,
Ribbons twirl in bright array.
Jupiter laughs, a playful giant,
While Mars forgot his belt, so defiant.

Comets zoom with silly grace,
Spinning wildly in cosmic race.
The stars giggle as they spin,
While Earth's onlookers grin and spin.

Asteroids dance with clumsy flair,
Each one grumbles a cosmic dare.
The Milky Way, a long parade,
Where every twinkle's charm is made.

And Neptune waves from far away,
Winking at each wobbly sway.
Oh, stardust dreams in moonlit night,
Turn troubles into laughter's flight.

Dance of the Astral Bands

Planets groove in cosmic bands,
Swinging through the starry lands.
Venus tripled in her shoes,
Wobbling with cosmic blues.

Uranus twirls in a bizarre jig,
Sweeping moons like a dancing twig.
With each spin, they chuckle loud,
Creating a merry, celestial crowd.

Shooting stars, the crowd pleasers,
Zipping by like playful sneezers.
The sun's a DJ, spinning tunes,
As planets boogie 'neath the moons.

In this far-off galaxy bright,
Everyone's laughing with delight.
So come and join this silly spree,
In the dance of cosmic glee!

Celestial Whispers

Stars tell tales in hushed delight,
Of cosmic pranks at dead of night.
Mercury's always in a rush,
While Mars makes mischief with a push.

Galaxies spin with clumsy grace,
As comets chase in a dizzy race.
Nebulas giggle in swirling hues,
While black holes snicker at shared views.

Planets whisper jokes so sweet,
As they orbit in a rhythm neat.
The cosmos hums a silly song,
Making sure the fun stays strong.

So stretch your ears to starry chimes,
Where laughter echoes through the times.
Each twinkle holds a burst of cheer,
In the vastness, funny vibes appear.

Orbiting Verses

In orbits round, the laughter flies,
With witty jokes in starlit skies.
Each planet spins a tale to tell,
Of cosmic antics they know so well.

Saturn grins with rings so wide,
While moons chase tails like playful pride.
Asteroids chuckle, dodging beams,
Joining the fun in far-off dreams.

Cosmic winds bring laughter's call,
As starlight dances, and shadows fall.
With every turn and twist of fate,
The universe sways, it's never late.

So raise a toast amongst the stars,
To giggles shared from Venus to Mars.
Each orbit spins a verse so bright,
A testament to joyous flight.

Ring of Enchantment

In a swirl of dust and ice, they whirl,
Dancing in the cosmic twirl.
A cat in space tried to meow,
But got lost in a giant cloud!

A wink from a star, a giggle from Mars,
The planets laugh, they're all like stars.
A comet slips on its tail so slick,
And sends us all into a cosmic trick!

Satellites spin like plates on sticks,
Chasing asteroids, playing tricks.
Jupiter's storm, a silly sight,
Could it be a giant's pillow fight?

In this circus of the sky so neat,
Every planet has a funky beat.
With rings that twirl and a wink of glee,
Who knew space could be so silly?

Planetary Verses

Around the sun they spin and sway,
Each in their own funny way.
Mercury is impatient and fast,
Always late to the cosmic blast!

Venus wears a cloud of cream,
While Mars dons a red gleam.
Jupiter eats just too much gas,
While Saturn shows off its swirly class!

In the void, stars play tag,
With Pluto saying, "I'm not a rag!"
Neptune chuckles, deep in its blue,
"Watch me juggle, those asteroids too!"

Cosmic parties, oh what a sight,
Ganymede brought the snacks tonight.
With rings of joy and moons that dance,
They spin together in a cosmic prance!

Echoes of Infinity

In the void, echoes bounce and play,
Silly sounds light years away.
A black hole giggles, pulls you in,
While stars just laugh, it's all a win!

Galaxies swirl like cotton candy,
A creamy treat that's rather dandy.
Planets hop with joy so grand,
While comets sketch with a cosmic hand!

Each pulsar sends out a cheeky beep,
While meteors giggle as they leap.
Space is silly, a cosmic dance,
Where even light takes a playful chance!

With echoes of laughter filling the night,
The universe shines, oh what a sight!
Every twinkle hides a hilarious scheme,
In this vast, wacky space-faring dream!

Cosmic Reverberations

Bouncing starlight, what a show,
With echoes swirling fast and slow.
Asteroids play a game of tag,
  While aliens do a silly brag!

With each pulse from distant stars,
The universe hums, with laughter ours.
Galaxies whirl, in a dance so neat,
While meteorites go to a cosmic beat!

Saturn spins with rings of fun,
  Jokes in space for everyone!
A quasar quacks, a neutron laughs,
Creating giggles through the drafts!

From black holes to the bright sun's glow,
  Every twinkle tells a humorous flow.
In this vast cosmos, we embrace the cheer,
  For in the universe, all is near and dear!

Whispered Secrets of the Cosmos

In the vastness, whispers play,
Stars giggle in a merry way.
Jupiter's belly shook with glee,
As Saturn tossed confetti free.

Pluto rolled his eyes so bold,
While Venus shared a tale retold.
Laughter echoed through the night,
In this dance of cosmic light.

Neptune splashed with watery cheer,
Uranus spun with silly sneer.
Galaxies joined in the jest,
Starlit parties, simply the best!

Comets dashed with giggles bright,
Twinkling tales of sheer delight.
As meteors start their fiery slide,
We laugh and dance with stellar pride.

Lyrical Orbits

Orbits twist in silly roles,
Planets play like friendly shoals.
Mars threw a hopscotch in the dew,
While Mercury spun a waltz so true.

Ceres hummed a tune with zest,
Twirling asteroids, what a fest!
Jovian jokers in a race,
Smiles ablaze across their face.

Rings of laughter whirled around,
In this boundless, joyful sound.
Stars and comets, all unite,
To dance beneath the endless night.

Lyrical cosmic pranks arise,
While shooting stars paint up the skies.
A symphony of spacey fun,
In every corner, laughter's spun.

Chasing Celestial Shadows

I chased a shadow 'round the moon,
It giggled, sang a playful tune.
In cosmic hide-and-seek we'd play,
Until the dawn stole night away.

A meteor raced with silly glee,
Laughing hard, it tripped on me.
And while I stumbled, lost my way,
A black hole winked and said, "Oh hey!"

Stars in pajamas, ready to snooze,
Whispering tales, they'd never lose.
Venus, with a grin so wide,
Joined the chase with cosmic pride.

Shadows danced and twirled with flair,
Floating through the cosmic air.
A galactic giggle, a playful sight,
Chasing shadows till the morning light.

The Poetry of the Planets

Planets scribble rhymes in space,
Comets race with a smiling face.
Mars' red scribbles, bold and brash,
While Earth just wants a splash of splash.

Saturn tossed a ring so wide,
Jokingly, it whirled with pride.
Uranus chuckled, 'What a scene!'
As Neptune joined with laughter keen.

Starlit poems danced in air,
Spinning tales beyond compare.
Galaxies giggled, stars did hum,
In this cosmic rhythm, all was fun.

The universe, a stage to play,
With celestial jesters in array.
The poetry flows, a cosmic stream,
In laughter and light, a shared dream.

Divinity in the Dust

In the cosmic mess, there's quite a fuss,
Dust bunnies dance, join the stardust bus.
Planets in laughter, they whirl and twirl,
While comets in capes give a joyful swirl.

Asteroids chuckle, colliding with flair,
Giggles in space fill the cold cosmic air.
Nebulas giggling, bright colors do burst,
In this celestial circus, we all know who's first.

The Milky Way winks, a cosmic delight,
As meteors tumble, oh what a sight!
Galaxies grinning, in spirals they leap,
While aliens giggle, not a secret to keep.

So here's to the dust, the fun and the play,
Floating through space, we'll forever stay.
With starlit confetti, let's dance with glee,
In this whimsical void, just you and me.

Orbiting Verses

Round and round we go, a merry chase,
Spinning through time in a cosmic race.
Laughing at gravity, we take a dip,
With each silly orbit, we do a flip.

Jovial planets, they wiggle and shake,
Dancing with moons, what a crazy wake!
Shooting stars wink, with a playful pout,
As they zoom past, they'll shout and shout.

Galactic giggles in every direction,
Wobbling orbits, defying perfection.
With each new twist, a chuckle we share,
In the space-time wonder, there's fun in the air.

With comets in hats, such a sight to behold,
Orbiting verses, in laughter we fold.
So grab your telescope, let's see what we find,
With humor in space, we're one of a kind.

Starlit Circular Ballads

In circles we sing 'neath the starlit beam,
Whirling through the cosmos, chasing a dream.
With planets that giggle and comets that prance,
The universe jests in a cosmic dance.

The orbits are laughter, gravity's jest,
Sharing their tales, they all feel blessed.
Each twinkle a wink, a playful embrace,
As stars spin around in a dizzying race.

With rhymes that float on the solar breeze,
Jovial rhythms bring us to our knees.
Galaxies twirl in a colorful show,
While space-time chuckles, putting on a glow.

Starlit ballads echo through the night,
A cosmic symphony, pure delight.
So join in the fun, let's shimmy and cheer,
In the grand galactic fair, we'll all persevere.

Enigmatic Edge of the Universe

On the edge of the cosmos, a riddle they say,
Mysteries dance in a whimsical way.
With laughter erupting from strange cosmic sights,
As quasars giggle through magical nights.

The void holds secrets of comedy vast,
While pulsars tick-tock, their giggles are cast.
Antimatter winks, in peculiar glee,
At the edge of it all, it's just you and me.

Cosmic balloons float, full of hot air,
Astrophysics puzzled, in the humor we share.
Planets in twirls do their humorous spins,
As we chuckle aloud, inviting more wins.

So here at the fringe, let's frolic and play,
Embrace the absurdity, come what may!
With each strange comet, let's dance in delight,
At the enigmatic edge, we shine ever bright.

Orbital Secrets

In a swirl of dust, the planets play,
Spinning round their sun all day.
A comet sneezes, what a sight,
Waving little tails in flight.

Asteroids dance, a clumsy jig,
While a star giggles, it's not too big.
A meteorite trips on a moon,
Kicking up laughs, oh what a tune!

Galaxies swirl, giving a wink,
While black holes pout and mutter, I think.
Satellites gossip with whispers bright,
Sharing stories of their cosmic plight.

Floating in space, a celestial kite,
Bound to drift through the endless night.
The universe chuckles, full of charm,
In this canvas where no one can harm.

Cosmic Melodies

The stars hum softly, a jolly tune,
While planets waltz to the light of the moon.
A bass note rumbles from deep space pang,
As comets respond with a joyful clang.

Jupiter jiggles with gaseous grace,
While Venus tries to keep up the pace.
A harmonic chorus, each world a voice,
In this grand realm, we rejoice, rejoice!

Meteor showers make confetti bright,
Tickling the suns with laughter and light.
Orbits spin round like a merry-go-round,
Creating the music in waves all around.

In the cosmic ballroom, we all take a step,
Winking at galaxies, no room for regret.
Join the dance of celestial glee,
Lost in the rhythms of eternity.

Astral Journeys

A spaceship dreams of distant stars,
Wishing to frolic on the rings of Mars.
Adventurers laugh as they zoom past light,
Finding new snacks in the endless night.

Astro-kittens chase a shooting star,
Purring and leaping, oh so bizarre!
They team up with moonbeams in a race,
Sampling the cosmos, it's a wild place.

Galactic travelers munch on space pies,
While aliens giggle with twinkling eyes.
Each journey unfolds with wonders untold,
In the vastness where silliness unfolds.

A nebula offers a ride on its back,
Through whimsical trails and nebulous tracks.
Together they vow, in laughter we'll roam,
Creating new tales wherever we comb.

Celestial Tapestries

Woven in starlight, a fabric of fun,
Threads of the cosmos, each sparkling one.
A tapestry bright with colors galore,
Whispers of laughter echo evermore.

Stitches of planets, and comets embrace,
Sewing together this whimsical space.
With thread made of smiles, oh what a sight,
Each twinkle a joke, each shadow a light.

In this quilt of infinity, secrets unfold,
Giggles of galaxies, a joy to behold.
Nebulas swirl in a dance of delight,
As we share in the wonder of cosmic night.

So gather your laughter, your stardust, your bolts,
In the fabric of space, we'll find all our jolts.
For in the grand weave of the universe's game,
The more that we giggle, the more that we claim.

Harmonies of Asteroids

In space, a rock band starts to play,
Asteroids jamming in their own way.
They sing of comets, tails so bright,
And dance around in velvet night.

One rocky fella took a spill,
He spun around, oh what a thrill!
The others laughed as he went whizz,
In cosmic chaos, that's how it is.

A pebbly score began to rise,
With shooting stars as the surprise.
They played a tune, both wild and free,
A hit among the galaxy.

So if you look and hear a sound,
It's asteroid music spinning 'round.
A cosmic gig, oh what a sight,
In laughter sparkles, pure delight!

Celestial Fantasies

In the sky, where planets spin,
A little dreamer grins and grins.
He rides a rocket made of cheese,
With cosmic mice on tiny skis.

Galaxies twirl like cotton candy,
As stardust pets get quite dandy.
They twinkle on a silver plate,
And dance with comets, oh so great.

In tinfoil hats and glitter shoes,
They choose to play and not to lose.
A whimsical race around the stars,
In-beaming laughter, oh how bizarre!

With every twink, a joke is spun,
In cosmic realms, there's never one.
As laughter echoes through the skies,
The universe hums with happy sighs!

Galactic Stories

A timewarp tale of cosmic jest,
Where planets gather for a fest.
Neptune spins a yarn so wide,
With Uranus chuckling by his side.

The Milky Way sings songs of old,
With meteor showers, bright and bold.
They swap their stories, all the while,
Each twist makes even black holes smile.

The sun shares puns that light the way,
While moons roll on in humor's play.
And comets streak with jokes on tails,
As laughter echoes through the veils.

So grab a star, pull up a chair,
In galactic tales, you'll find some flair.
With every plot that does abound,
There's joy and giggles all around!

Stellar Echoes

In an echo chamber far away,
Stars giggle loud at the end of day.
They bounce their light in silly rhyme,
Creating shadows lost in time.

A pulsar winks with a cheeky grin,
While black holes cackle from within.
Neutron stars, they flicker and sway,
Playing tricks in a starry ballet.

As solar flares share jokes on beams,
Galaxies burst with giddy dreams.
The cosmos shakes with laughter's tune,
While space-time dances, night or noon.

So let us join this cosmic play,
With stellar echoes bright as day.
In laughs and lights, the fun ignites,
In every constellation's flights!

Augustus' Glittering Girdle

A belt of sparkles wide and bright,
Around the giant's waist they fight.
They laugh and dance, a cosmic brawl,
Dodging asteroids, having a ball.

The rings are like a fancy dress,
Swirling in space, oh what a mess!
They toss and twirl, these frozen flakes,
Making merry with every shake.

From icy rocks to dusty trails,
They giggle while the stardust sails.
It's a joyride in a galactic spree,
A shimmering party for you and me!

Oh Augustus, with your bling so grand,
You've got the best dance floor in the land.
So twirl and spin, there's no need to stop,
In your glittering girdle, we'll forever bop!

Harmony of the Gaseous Giant

Beneath the clouds, giggles arise,
Jokes bounce around like playful pies.
A gaseous realm, where laughter swells,
With whimsical winds and funny spells.

The storms of humor, they twist and twine,
Mirthful tempests that tickle and shine.
With every gust, the chuckles roar,
As the giant dances on the stellar floor.

Electric bolts go zapping by,
In the humor sphere, oh me, oh my!
Dancing farts of colorful gas,
Make cosmic jokes that never pass.

So come take part in this jolly spree,
In the gaseous giant, wild and free.
With every swirl, joy's on the rise,
Let's laugh together beneath the skies!

Luminous Loops of Wonder

In the cosmic circus, the loops do gleam,
With starlight sparkles, oh what a dream!
They swoop and swirl, a merry chase,
    Creating giggles in the vast space.

Twinkling darts through the hoops so grand,
    Playful rings that look so unplanned.
They zip and zoom, in a light-filled race,
Chasing sparkles in an endless embrace.

Each luminous loop, a joy-filled delight,
Flashes of laughter in the dead of night.
They tease the moons with a wink and a grin,
    In this circus of light, let the fun begin!

So join the dance in this stellar show,
Where the loops of wonder endlessly flow.
With every twist and a burst of cheer,
In luminous laughter, let's persevere!

Spheres of Light and Shadow

Round and round, the spheres play hide,
In a game of tag, while stars collide.
Giggles echo through the night,
A dance of shadows, sheer delight.

The moons can't stop their silly jive,
Bobbing and weaving, oh how they thrive!
They peek and pop, a humorous sight,
Dancing in tandem with beams of light.

Shadowed splashes in radiant play,
Creating laughter that's here to stay.
With every twirl, the cosmos beams,
Spheres of joy, unraveling dreams.

So let's lift off to the cosmic ball,
Where laughter spins and shadows fall.
In this merry round, we'll dance forever,
In spheres of light, we'll be clever together!

Ethereal Echoes

In the night sky, a donut spins,
A cosmic treat, where laughter begins.
Around it go, the stars just tease,
Making wishes as they float with ease.

A comet whizzes, a wink and a nod,
While asteroids dance, it seems like a fraud.
The universe giggles, it's quite absurd,
As planets play tag, unheard but served.

Galaxies swirl in a jelly-like haze,
Creating a party where spacers can blaze.
With fizzing stardust and twinkling tales,
We'll toast to the cosmos; it never fails.

So grab your telescope, aim for the fun,
Where the celestial antics have only begun.
In the vast open sky, humor collides,
As laughter echoes where the starlight resides.

Mystic Orbits

Planets in hats, spinning round with cheer,
They twirl and they whirl, with a cheerleader's sneer.
With rings made of sprinkles, a carnival glow,
The galaxy's circus puts on quite a show.

Meteor showers, a squishy delight,
Confetti of stardust, a glorious sight.
Each blip in the shop, a galactic satire,
As comets roll by with a whoosh and a wire.

In the cosmic café, they serve up a brew,
Of Milky Way lattes with whipped Dream Star too.
The black holes giggle, though they keep it discreet,
While aliens dance to an intergalactic beat.

So let's toast to the stars, with a wink and a shout,
In the funny old cosmos, there's never a doubt.
The universe chuckles, it brings us good cheer,
As we spiral on through, with laughter sincere.

Comet's Caress

A comet slides in with a fuzzy mustache,
Waving at moons with a whimsical flash.
"Catch me if you can," it sings with glee,
As it zooms past planets, wild and free.

Asteroids giggle, doing a jig,
While a shooting star makes the night feel big.
It twirls and it curls, in a twinkling spree,
A cosmic conga, as jolly as can be.

Galactic balloons float high in the air,
While meteors serve up their popcorn with flair.
Each flicker of light tells a joke in disguise,
As laughter erupts from the vast inky skies.

With each cosmic wink, let's celebrate fate,
In the grand universe, we'll dance and we'll skate.
For every bright twitch leads to joy just above,
A comical jaunt, wrapped in starlit love.

Cosmic Cornucopia

A basket of laughter, the cosmos provides,
With plump little planets and snickering tides.
The stars all chuckle, a glimmering crew,
As space-time jangles its joyful debut.

Meteorites bounce on a chocolate-dipped world,
While nebulae flutter with colors unfurled.
A lazy black hole takes a break for a snack,
With sprinkles and giggles, it's always on track.

Galaxies twirl in a hula-hoop dance,
As gravity pulls in a whimsical chance.
Rings that are funky and moons in a spin,
Celebrate laughter—let the fun times begin!

So gather your friends, let's shoot for the stars,
Where the wackiest wonders glide past in their cars.
In the cosmic cornucopia, it's all a delight,
With a punchline of planets, we'll party tonight!

Cosmic Dance of Debris

A rock in space does a little spin,
While calling out, "Hey, where have you been?"
The dust clouds giggle, floating on by,
As some stop to joke about the night sky.

A comet sneezes, creating a trail,
While meteors shout, "Why don't we sail?"
They laugh at the stars, who twinkle with glee,
As the universe sways in celestial spree.

Each fragment jives with a shimmering flair,
Making sure all their movement is rare.
With cosmic waltzes, they spin and they twirl,
What a funny dance in this vast, endless swirl!

So here in the void, with a chuckle so bright,
The debris finds joy in the laughter of night.
In this frolicsome space, they take their stance,
And we all are invited to join in the dance!

Echoes of the Asteroid Belt

In the belt of rocks, they throw a great bash,
While dodging each other, oh what a clash!
One says, "I'm large!" another replies,
"But I'm much smaller! Just look at my size!"

They play hide and seek in the cosmic maze,
Chirping and giggling in playful ways.
With every little bump, their laughter ignites,
As they swirl around in their asteroid nights.

The asteroids sing in a clunky line,
"Watch me, watch me! Look how I shine!"
One rolls with style, another just flips,
They all strike a pose, giving each other quips.

So if you should wander through space nice and slow,
You might hear their echoes, a comical show.
With playful delight, they keep on their trek,
Making sure the cosmos has a laugh on deck!

Frozen Dreams of the Gas Giant

In a world of gases, a chilly delight,
The clouds start to giggle in the dim twilight.
One cloud proclaimed, "I'm the fluffiest here!"
While the others broke down in a laughter so sheer.

They drift through the skies in a shimmering dance,
With frosty little whispers, they share every chance.
One cloud took a dip, just to feel the chill,
And exclaimed, "Oh dear! This is such a thrill!"

When winds play their tricks, they all swirl about,
And bubble up stories, with a giggling shout.
"Let's freeze a comet!" squeals one with glee,
"Or slide on a ring—come on, follow me!"

So off they all go into the vast unknown,
Making frozen dreams that twirl and have grown.
In this chilly expanse, a joyful brigade,
With laughter and light through the stars they cascade!

Enchanted Haloes

In the phantom of night, the halo glows bright,
While moonbeams and giggles converge in delight.
A little fairy shouts, "Catch the light show!"
While rings around planets begin their own flow.

With colors that twinkle like laughter in glee,
They swerve and they twirl, oh, the harmony!
With glittering trails that tease and entwine,
The halo's a canvas of humor divine.

A star tumbled down, took a swirl with a wink,
"I'm just practicing for my cosmic drink!"
While each scattered spark adds to the fun,
In this stellar pageant, they've only begun!

So gather 'round, friends, for a whimsical spree,
Where halos and laughter collide joyfully.
In the realm of the stars, take your chance to roam,
As the universe dances, let it feel like home!

Frozen Elegies

In space, ice cream cones spin tight,
Galactic giggles take flight.
Snowflakes dance with a twinkling flail,
Aliens cheer with a frozen pail.

Stars toss snow like they own the show,
While comets glide in a frosty flow.
Laughing moons roll in cosmic delight,
As planets wear hats made of starlight.

A penguin waltz with a twist so slick,
With a space whale doing a stellar kick.
Frosty friends in a jovial race,
Trying to keep up in the chilly space.

So here's to the ice, the stars, the fun,
Where even the sun can't help but run.
Join the laughter, take a seat,
In this funny cosmos, oh so sweet!

Celestial Ballet

In a tutu, the moon takes a spin,
While the stars chuckle, wearing a grin.
Planets line up for the grand debut,
In a cosmic ballet, oh what a view!

Shooting stars slide, a dazzling display,
With each twirl, they shimmer and sway.
Galaxies whirl with a spin and a bop,
As asteroids jiggle and never stop.

Comets pirouette with a tail of delight,
Surely it's wrong, but it feels just right.
With black holes clapping, a rhythm so grand,
Every celestial body joins in the band.

Bravo, dear universe, laugh till you're done,
For there's never a dull moment when dancing with fun!
Jump in this whirl, it's a twinkle-filled spree,
Where laughter and light are wild and free!

Reflective Reveries

In the mirror of stars, reflections play,
Silly giggles echo where shadows sway.
Nebulae ponder their fluffy delight,
As they shimmer and giggle through endless night.

Dreamy dawns with sunbeam ties,
Catch playful whispers from comet spies.
A cosmic joke on the edge of time,
Where starlight dances in a clumsy rhyme.

Planets joke while they orbit near,
Singing soft songs only they can hear.
With each twist and turn, they giggle and spin,
Creating new worlds where merriment's kin.

So raise your glass of meteor dust,
Toast to the cosmos, the fun is a must!
In this mirrored realm of whimsical cheer,
Each shared laughter makes the universe clear!

Heavenly Circlets

Rings of laughter wrap 'round the moons,
As they twirl and dance to whimsical tunes.
Each little planet, a jester in sight,
Spreading joy in a galactic flight.

Meteorites fall like confetti in play,
While the sun cracks jokes, come join the fray!
Even black holes can't help but grin,
As they swirl and spin, inviting in.

Comets bring cheese for a galactic feast,
While stardust tickles, it's laughter at least.
In this space of whimsy, all float and sway,
With celestial friends, we'll laugh all day.

So don your best grin, let the joy be profound,
In these heavenly circlets, we're happily bound!
Hold hands with the stars, let your spirit ignite,
As we twinkle with laughter, all through the night!

www.ingramcontent.com/pod-product-compliance
Lightning Source LLC
Chambersburg PA
CBHW051639160426
43209CB00004B/716